I Feel...

ALLERGIC

Words and pictures by

DJ Corchin

Sometimes my skin **itches**

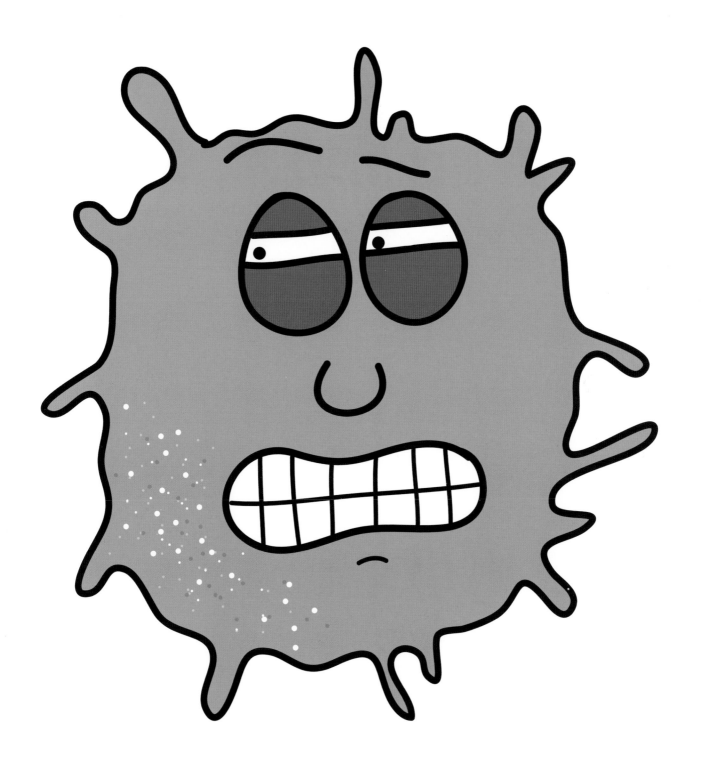

'cause I **play** in the grass.

Or I **drink** too much milk

and get **really** bad gas.

I can't **eat** the cupcakes they give out in class.

I have a small quirk
where I just have to **pass**.

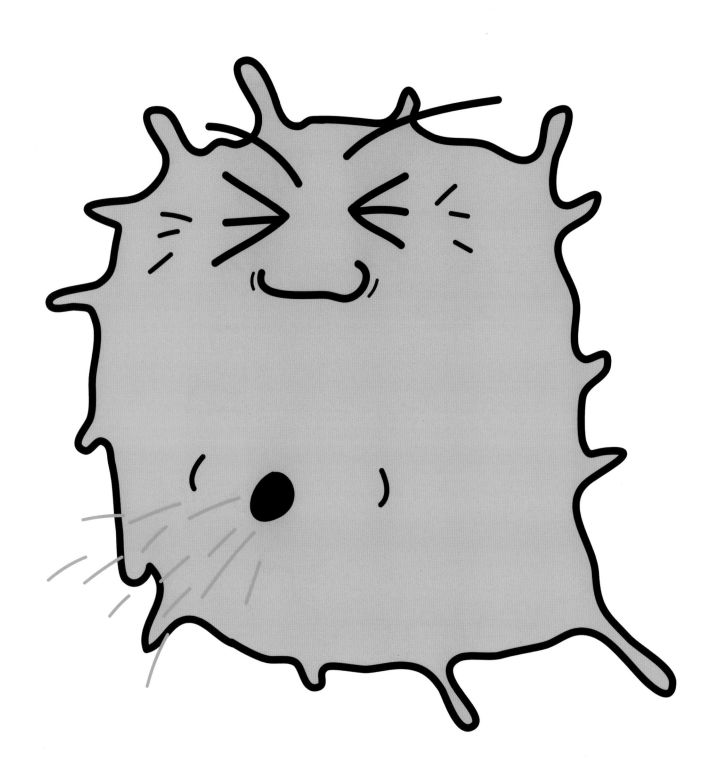

I **sneeze** myself silly

from Zuzu, your **cat**.

My eyes can't stop **watering**

from your grandpa's **wool** hat.

We might be just having
a casual **chat,**

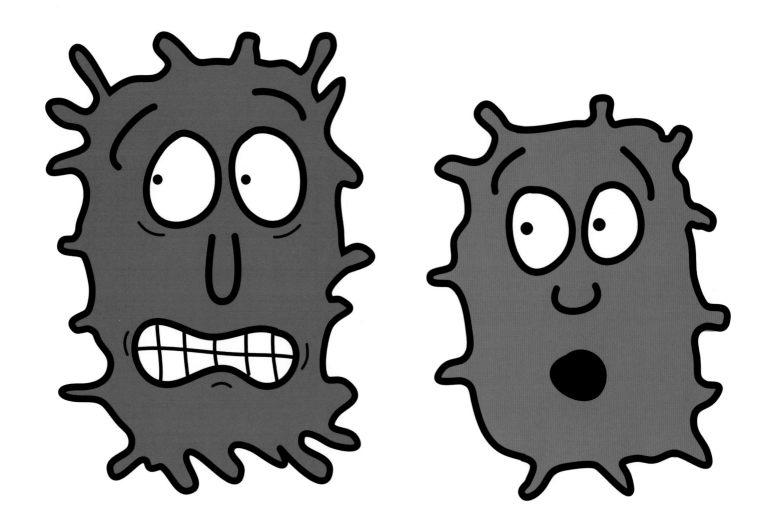

but **inside** I'm thinking where the bathrooms are at.

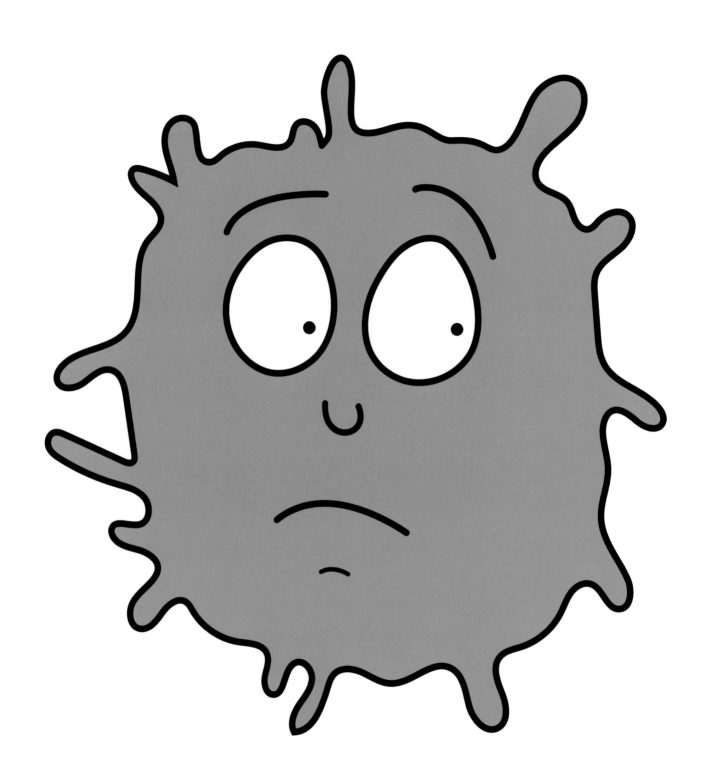

I can't go outside
to **ride** my new bike

'cause the sun **hurts** my skin
when I'm taking a hike.

Sometimes I can't **eat** all the things that I like.

They might make me **red**

or my blood sugar **spike**.

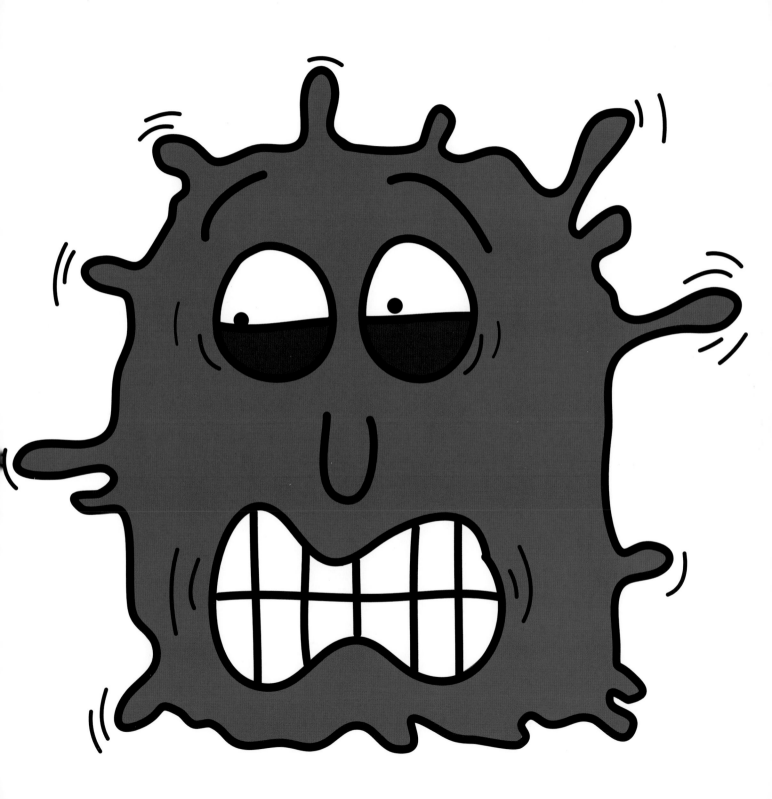

Sometimes it's much worse,
like if I **eat** a small nut.

It becomes **hard** to breathe and my throat starts to shut.

If I'm **stung** by a bee
my face might swell up,

and I'll need to get help before my tongue **thwah thoo thupths.**

Sometimes my **allergies** can change all my plans.

But they **never** can stop me or **change** who I am.

As I **discover** my quirks,
there's one thing I've known:

All the friends that I meet
have **quirks** of their own.

I Feel...
ALLERGIC

Allergies are part of our lives, but they can't stop us from being who we are.

There are so many types of allergies. Some of them are inconvenient but don't affect someone's life too much. Some of them have a major impact on the things we can do every day and can make us feel left out. Here are some discussion topics and activities to help!

Allergy Flashcards

There are many different types of allergies a person can have. Make flashcards to learn about them and about other people who have them.

1. Obtain a pack of plain index cards or make your own out of recycled paper or construction paper.

2. Make a list of all the types of allergies you can think of, starting with ones that your friends and family may have told you about.

3. Either with a caring adult or with tools you're allowed to use, you can look up more types of allergies on the internet.

4. On one side of each index card, write the name of the allergy, including the scientific name if you can find it, or a basic name like "Nut Allergy" or "Sun Allergy."

5. On the other side, write a description of what the allergy is, what can trigger it, and what can happen if it's triggered, plus any other information about it that is helpful.

6. If there's room on the index card, draw an I Feel... face showing how someone might feel when the allergy is triggered.

I Feel... achoooo!

Having a serious allergy isn't always about what you can and can't do. Sometimes it's about how your restrictions can make you feel. It's important to talk about and explore those feelings. Find a friend or trusted adult and use these questions to start a conversation:

1. What are some activities you can't do or foods you can't eat because of your allergy?

2. How does it make you feel when that happens?

3. What are some things you wish your friends knew about your allergy?

4. What are some things you wish your friends would help with?

5. What can you do to feel better when you feel that way inside?

6. Who can you talk to if you are feeling sad or angry?

Celebrating Friends

This activity is for a friend who shared with you that they have a food allergy.

1. If your friend is OK with it, have a discussion about their allergy.

2. Be sure to listen to what they can and cannot do.

3. Take note of how they feel when they can't do something because of their allergy.

4. Plan a special meal celebrating your friendship by making a list of all of their favorite foods that they can eat. Ask your friend and their parents if it would be OK for you to make one of those foods or bring it to the friendship party.

5. Make it a fun event with games you like to play, movies you like to watch, and more.

It is ALWAYS OK to ask someone for help when you are feeling bad.

The I Feel... Children's Series is a resource created to assist in discussions about emotional awareness.

Please seek the help of a trained mental healthcare professional and start a discussion today.